The first electric railway to be opened in the United Kingdom was Magnus Volk's short line along the Brighton seafront, opened on August Bank Holiday 1883.

EARLY ELECTRIC TRAINS

R. L. Vickers

Shire Publications Ltd

CONTENTS

Printed in Great Britain by C. I. Thomas & Sons (Haverfordwest) Ltd, Press Buildings, Merlins Bridge, Haverfordwest, Dyfed SA61 1XF.

British Library Cataloguing in Publication Data: Vickers, R. L. (Ray L). Early electric trains. I. Title. 385.363. ISBN 0-7478-0136-3.

ACKNOWLEDGEMENTS
I appreciate and acknowledge the help given me by all those who supplied prints and information. Especial thanks go to Dr I. D. O. Frew for reading and commenting on my typescript, and to Ms Lynn Kilgarriff for typing it. I must thank Messrs W. K. Donald, R. L. Skelton and J. K. Wright for constructive comments, which have been incorporated in this book. Any errors in this work are solely my responsibility.
Illustrations are acknowledged as follows: Brighton Reference Libraries, pages 1 and 6 (bottom); Colourail/T. J. Edgington, cover; GEC-Alsthom, pages 8 (bottom) and 10; Lens of Sutton, pages 5, 8 (top), 11 (bottom), 12 (both), 14 (both), 19, 20 (both), 22 (bottom), 24, 25 (top), 26 (top and centre), 27 (bottom), 28 (top), 30 (all), 31 (top) and 32; Locomotive Publishing Company, page 24; London Borough of Croydon, page 25 (bottom); London Transport Museum, pages 4, 7 (top), 15, 16 (both), 17, 18 (both), 21 (bottom), 26 (bottom), 27 (top), 28 (bottom) and 29 (both); Mather and Platt Limited, page 6 (top); National Museums and Galleries on Merseyside, pages 7 (bottom) and 22 (second from bottom); National Railway Museum, pages 11 (centre), 13 (Horwich Collection) and 23; Newcastle upon Tyne City Libraries, page 21 (top); R. Powell-Hendry, page 31 (bottom); Real Photographs, pages 11 (top) and 22 (top two); Ulster Museum, R. J. Welch Collection, page 2; R. L. Vickers, page 9.

Cover: *Liverpool Overhead Railway train number 20 entering St James Street station in October 1956, a few months before the railway closed on 31st December 1956.*

Below: *The Giant's Causeway, Portrush and Bush Valley Railway and Tramway Company opened in September 1883. Motored car number 7 is seen here at Dunluce Castle with passengers and crew. The iron rail at the trackside is the conducting rail. The gap caused by the farm gate is bridged by a cable connection. This unique electrical system was replaced by a 500 volts overhead cable in 1899.*

THE FIRST ELECTRIC TRAINS

The first experimental electric locomotives were developed almost simultaneously with the steam locomotive. The first public inter-city steam railway was the Liverpool and Manchester Railway of 1830. The next year Michael Faraday discovered some of the fundamental principles of electricity. These principles were put to use in 1835, when Thomas Davenport demonstrated a small model electric motor in New England. In Scotland Robert Davidson built a model electric car in 1837, followed in 1842 by a full-scale electric locomotive, the *Galvani*, tested on the Edinburgh to Glasgow main line. In Bath that year a Mr Porter built a small electric car on the same principles as the *Galvani*. The *Galvani* used electricity from batteries. Copper and zinc plates were 'burnt' in strong acid, the chemical reactions eating away the zinc to produce new compounds and electrical current. Faraday estimated that electricity could never compete with steam, because of the great cost of 'burning' metals in acid compared to burning coal in a boiler. The point was lost on some Scottish enginemen, who smashed the *Galvani*, fearing it could threaten their jobs.

In the United States battery-powered locomotives were built. Some were of great power. The most successful one ran in tests along the Baltimore and Ohio Railroad main line, at speeds comparable to those of steam locomotives. It used batteries called 'Grove's cells' as they were invented by Sir William Robert Grove, who was both a judge and a physicist. Grove's cells were made with platinum. Not surprisingly, the locomotive was expensive to run, forty times more so than a comparable steam engine.

However, the most important developments took place outside the locomotive industry. The telegraph and electroplating industries developed rapidly from the 1840s. As they grew, they created markets for electrical equipment, such as pure copper wires and accurate meters for measuring power, voltages and so on. These materials had not been available to the pioneers. Faraday is said to have used bent hat pins in experiments because good wire was difficult to get.

As important as new technology was the concept of a railway as an interdependent complex with power cheaply generated at a central point, then distributed to vehicles along the track, every part dependent upon the others. The idea had been pioneered by the early 'atmospheric' railway, which failed. The new system depended upon a reliable source of cheap electric power, and so the modern electric railway was impossible until the 1860s. Then, many inventors working independently developed the dynamo, which produced low-voltage (electrical pressure), high-amperage (power) direct current (DC). Direct current, produced by batteries, dynamos and electric eels, is current that flows in one direction only. Later, high-voltage alternators were developed. These produce a current that changes, that is alternates, its direction at regular intervals.

Dynamos produced ample electricity, but there was still need of a motor. The primitive electro-magnetic motors used in the early days were incapable of developing high power. However, in the 1860s Dr Werner von Siemens of Germany discovered that the dynamo could be operated as a motor. When mechanical power was put in, it generated electricity, but when electrical power was fed in, it acted as a motor, developing mechanical power.

Dr Siemens built the first electric railway to incorporate all the characteristics of modern electric railway systems, namely a central generator, an electrical distribution network and a locomotive that picked up power from the network instead of making its own power. These three parts interlocked to make a system in which every part was dependent upon the others.

This railway system was demonstrated at the Berlin Exposition of 1879. It was rather like a large toy trainset, with a very small locomotive and carriages upon which passengers sat. The electric current was distributed along the two tracks, returning to earth via a central rail. This railway was small enough to be packed up and sent all over Europe on display. It came to London in 1881, the year a full-size working tramway was opened in Berlin. In the United States Thomas Edison was making small electric locomotives.

Important commercial electric railways were opened in Britain in 1883, at opposite ends of the British Isles. The first to open was at Brighton, on the August Bank Holiday. Still working, it is probably the oldest electric railway in the world. It was built by Brighton Corporation's Electrical Engineer, Magnus Volk. The original line was only a quarter-mile (400 metres) long and 2 foot (610 mm) gauge but proved so popular that it was rebuilt to a length of 1³/₄ miles (2.8 km) and a gauge of 2 feet 8¹/₂ inches (826 mm), the characteristics it has today. Some of the original cars lasted until the 1930s.

The other railway was in Northern Ireland. The Portrush, Bush Valley and Giant's Causeway Tramway and Railway Company was the world's longest electric railway when opened in September 1883. It was both tramway and railway, as the difference between the two is legal, not technical. Being laid upon a public road, a tramway shares its track with others, whilst a railway has exclusive rights of way. Work had begun some years before. It had been planned to use a system similar to the German ones, namely feeding current along the tracks to the cars. It was soon found that the current dissipated after about 2 miles (3 km). So the current was fed along a heavily insulated third rail, placed alongside the track like a fence. In the towns this third rail could not be used, so steam trams were bought for use in Portrush until in 1899 the system was replaced by an overhead wire at 500 volts. The railway worked until closure in 1948.

Also in Ulster was the Bessbrook and Newry Tramway, opened in 1885, and worked electrically from then until closure in 1949. The two lines together gave Ireland a total of 10 miles (16 km) of electric railway by 1886, a world record, but it did not last for long, as in North America great developments were soon to take place, associated with Frank Julian Sprague, the father of the modern electric train.

Sprague improved the method of collecting current from overhead wires and developed a small but powerful electric motor, which he attached directly to the axle, with part of the weight borne by a 'nose' suspended from the vehicle body. This motor and suspension system made possible electric trains that could work on lightly laid track. By the 1890s America was crisscrossed with tramways and 'inter-urban' electric railways.

Sprague's most important invention, in 1898, was the system of multiple unit control, that is trains of powered carriages, all controlled from a single driving cab. This not only cut wage bills, it also improved acceleration and braking, enabling long fast trains to be run safely and reliably. The multiple unit (MU) system made Sprague a millionaire, made the electric trains superior to any other form of suburban rail traction, such as steam or cable cars, and gave American firms many years' lead over competitors. But in Britain many electric railways had already been built by British or continental firms.

City and South London Railway locomotive number 1 and train at Stockwell depot. The coaches were called 'padded cells' by the passengers, because they were so small and almost windowless. The first Tube carriages did not have windows, as it was assumed that passengers would not want to look out when there was nothing to see.

Windows were added later to new CSLR carriages, as shown here. Note also the carriage entrance gates, which were a feature of London Tube trains from the 1890s until the 1920s.

BRITISH TECHNOLOGY

Even in Victorian times, London had road traffic problems. Congestion was as bad in major provincial cities. There was an obvious need for efficient transport, and electric trains were the answer.

London had the world's first deep-level electric Tube, and soon afterwards Liverpool had the world's first elevated electric railway. The Tube was the City and South London Railway (CSLR), designed to use cable haulage. A moving endless cable was gripped by a special device in the cars, and thereby dragged along. The same principle is still used by the San Francisco cable cars and the Great Orme Tramway in Llandudno, Gwynedd.

Unfortunately for the CSLR, its cable suppliers went bankrupt, leaving a railway company with a half-built Tube stretching from Southwark to the City. As electric trains had worked well in Ireland, it was suggested that perhaps they could do equally well underneath London. The electric equipment came from Mather and Platt of Manchester, who employed as adviser Dr John Hopkinson, the leading Brit-

ish electrical expert and consultant to the Giant's Causeway Line.

Very strict conditions were imposed on Mather and Platt by the desperate CSLR. Mather and Platt had to guarantee running costs would not exceed $3^{1}/_{2}$d per train mile and were totally responsible for the railway for two years from the date of signing the contract, in February 1889. The conditions were met and beaten. The railway opened in December 1890 and it made profits, though not large ones as it suffered from tramway competition. Train sizes were limited because of the small tunnels and because there were sharp gradients and steep curves. These conditions remained until the railway was rebuilt in the 1920s and joined to the Northern Line. The original City terminus at King William Street was closed in 1900, to be replaced by the Bank junction.

The Liverpool Overhead Railway was erected in 1893, using advice from J. H. Greathead, an engineer to the CSLR. The electric trains used were built by Dick, Kerr and Company of Preston, one of the British

5

Above: *A close-up view of an original CSLR locomotive. After withdrawal, two were preserved, but one was destroyed by a bomb in the Blitz. The survivor is in the Science Museum.*

Below: *Volk's Brighton and Rottingdean Seashore Electric Railway ran for 2³/4 miles (4.4 km). The single carriage was carried on four legs that straddled two separate tracks, 18 feet (5.5 metres) apart. At high tide the tracks were covered in 15 feet (4.6 metres) of sea water. Electric power came from a wire on the shore via trolley arms on the car. This odd contraption worked well between 1896 and 1901, when the railway was closed to make way for sea defences.*

pioneers of electric traction. In 1918 Dick, Kerr of Preston, Siemens Brothers Limited of Stafford, Phoenix Dynamo of Bradford and Willans and Robinson of Rugby amalgamated to form the English Electric Company, which supplied much equipment for inter-war electric railways.

The Liverpool Overhead cars ran originally in two-car, later in three-car sets, the driver's controls in the front cab being connected to those in the rear cab by cables in a primitive multiple unit (MU) system, which meant that no more than three cars could be worked together in a train. All the cars were continually rebuilt and refurbished, with new bodies and engines. Before the Overhead closed in 1956, some cars had bodies like contemporary motor buses. One railcar has been restored to its original condition and is preserved in Liverpool Museum.

Dick, Kerr also supplied equipment to the Waterloo and City Line. This line, called the 'Drain' by generations of City commuters, was built by a main-line company, the London and South Western Rail-

6

The Waterloo and City Railway was a subsidiary of the LSWR which used British and American rolling stock. Shown here is number 15, an example of the five double-cabbed single-car sets which ran off-peak services. This car, one of a series 13-17, was supplied in 1899. More stock came in 1904 and 1922. All the stock, numbers 1-36 inclusive, was scrapped in 1940.

The Liverpool Overhead Railway was opened in 1893. It had the first electrically operated signals in Britain, and from 1921 it was the first railway in Britain with daylight colour-light signals. New cars came in 1896, and more new trailers later. The cars were fitted with new motors from 1902, so as to compete with tramway services. This is motor car number 25, one of the original fifteen two-car sets of 1893. Built of teakwood, it is shown here with a three-car train.

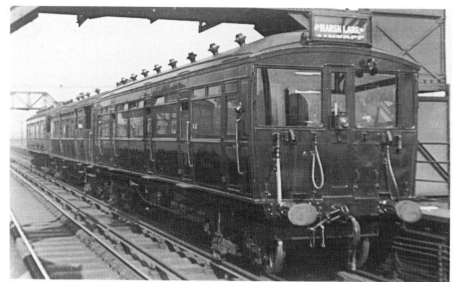

The Lancashire and Yorkshire Railway ran joint services from Southport to Dingle with the Liverpool Overhead Railway. The lightweight cars used aluminium panelling on their bodies. Joint LYR-LOR services operated from 1906 to 1914, these cars later being used on workmen's specials and local services. They were withdrawn in 1945, scrapped in 1946. The cars ran either singly or, as here, coupled into trains. The lead vehicle is motor third 28696.

The experimental three-car set made for the Holcombe Brook to Bury branch, photographed before the overhead was dismantled in 1918. The three-car set was later fitted with a diesel engine and generator and worked experimentally on the Blackpool Central to Lytham service in 1928/9.

8

The unique 1200 volts DC side-rail system of the Bury to Manchester line. The conductor rail was normally covered with a hardwood surround, leaving a gap for the pickup as at A, but here the rail B is shown exposed, the wood surrounds C having fallen off. The system was dismantled to make way for the Manchester Light Railway in 1991.

way (LSWR), to connect its terminus at Waterloo with the City of London (Bank station). The line was completed in 1898. In operation, it used British and American trains. The American cars were made by Jackson and Sharp of Wilmington, Delaware, shipped in pieces from America, then assembled in the LSWR works at Eastleigh, Hampshire, into four-car units. Dick, Kerr in 1899 built some single cars for off-peak use, spare trailers coming in 1904 from the Preston Tramway Company. The entire line was re-equipped in 1940, the replacement trains lasting until modernisation in the early 1990s.

Dick, Kerr and Company also supplied the first electric locomotive to run in Ireland (as distinct from railcars). This was sold to the Dublin and Lacan Valley Tramway in 1907. The Dick, Kerr company was supplier to the major electrification schemes done by the Lancashire and Yorkshire Railway (LYR) around Liverpool and Manchester.

The Liverpool system opened first, in 1904. The lines had been electrified and a power station built within a few months, spurred on by competition with the North Eastern Railway (NER). The LYR won, opening one day before the NER, but the LYR line soon closed for repairs, reopening permanently on 13th May 1904.

Between 1905 and 1913 the system expanded to form an inverted A centred on Liverpool Exchange station, with one arm going to Southport, another to Ormskirk, and a connecting line forming the bar of the A. Three kinds of sets were used: a flat-topped stock on the Southport line; an elliptical-roofed design on the Ormskirk service; and a special lightweight aluminium-bodied stock made for use on joint services with the Liverpool Overhead Railway.

In 1912 a shunting locomotive was built for use in the Aintree marshalling yards. The axles and frames came from a steam-engine design, but electric motors were put into an ugly boxy body. The motors turned the wheels by means of a connecting link or 'jackshaft'. This was the only locomotive ever to use this drive on a British railway, although it was quite common elsewhere. The locomotive was a failure. It was withdrawn around 1922, but nobody knows its eventual fate.

Aintree is also famous for horse-racing. On days of the Grand National steeplechase two electric cars would be placed at either end of a long train, up to twelve carriages long. Multiple unit cables would be run along the train to form one giant electric multiple unit (EMU).

The original LYR cars ran until the 1930s, to be replaced by new London Midland and Scottish Railway (LMS) designs, themselves replaced in the 1980s. None of the original cars has been preserved, but an LMS set has been repainted in LMS colours and runs on special occasions.

Only a concrete block remains of the next LYR scheme. This block, near Bury, was the base of a pylon carrying over 3000 volts. The line, from Holcombe Brook to Bury, was electrified at this high voltage as

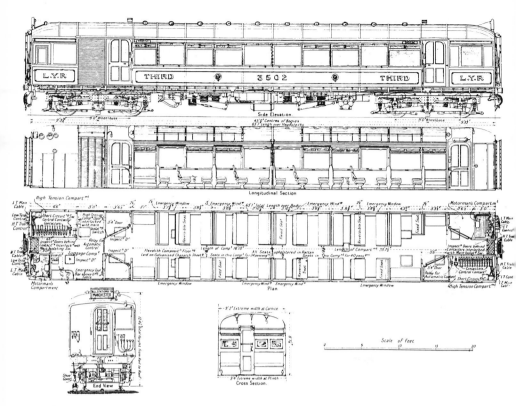

Diagram of the all-metal motor third car built in 1915 for the 1200 volts DC Manchester-Bury service, which started operating in April 1916.

part of a trial done by Dick, Kerr and Company, who were seeking an export order from Brazil. They electrified the line at their own expense to publicise their products, in return for which the LYR promised to buy Dick, Kerr equipment on any future electric scheme. Unfortunately neither the LYR nor the Brazilians were impressed by the scheme.

However, the LYR saw that high voltages had advantages, so when the line from Manchester to Bury was electrified a unique 1200 volt side-rail system was used. The original cars used were renowned for comfort and reliability. They survived until 1959, when they were replaced by a new type, the Class 504, two-car prototypes of the three-car Class 304 series used between Liverpool, Crewe and Manchester.

In south London and in Morecambe another system was tried, of German design, utilising high-voltage alternating current (AC). The Morecambe scheme was a successful experiment by the Midland Railway, but no major schemes were carried out by that company. Very similar technology was used by the London, Brighton and South Coast Railway (LBSCR) on an extensive system opened in 1909. This served the south London suburbs but was part of a plan to electrify the company's main line to Brighton. The very high voltage would have required few expensive electrical substations along the route. The electrical equipment and designs came from AEG of Berlin, but the LBSCR stipulated that as much material as possible should come from British firms, so AEG subcontracted

Top: *A five-car train of Manchester-Bury stock, shown at Bury sidings in the mid 1930s.*

Centre: *The LYR electric locomotive had pickups and pantographs so it could run on the LYR lines to Southport and Ormskirk, but it normally worked between Aintree sorting sidings and North Mersey Yard on transfer duties. It is shown here with such a freight train. The machine was a disappointment and was withdrawn in 1920.*

Bottom: *The Midland Railway tried out a very high-voltage AC system on the short Lancaster-Morecambe-Heysham line. It opened for service in 1908. This picture shows one of the 1908 two-car sets. The line was de-electrified in 1951, but re-electrified from 1952 with different rolling stock to try out equipment for BR's main lines. Regular passenger services began in 1953, but the line closed in 1966.*

11

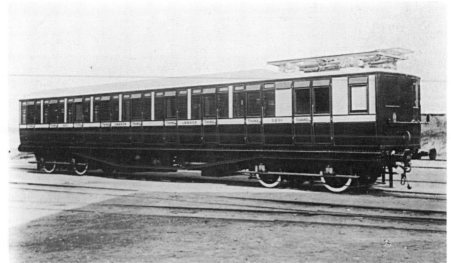

The London, Brighton and South Coast Railway used a similar high-voltage system to the Midland. Three-car trains were run, a first-class trailer between two third-class motor driving cars, which also had a guard's compartment each. The wooden bodies had metal underframes and extensive metal sheeting to earth the current in case of accidents. All cars were painted a smart umber brown and cream.

The weak point of the LBSCR system was the number and cost of the cantilevers needed to hold up the electric wires. As can be seen, they were very substantial pieces of metal, and it proved difficult to mass-produce them and so cut costs.

The Lancashire and Yorkshire Railway had one main-line electric locomotive. It is shown here under construction at Horwich Works c.1912. It had four 150 horsepower electric motors placed on the frames of a standard 2-4-2T shunter.

almost all the work to British companies. Originally opened from 1st December 1909 between London Bridge and Victoria, the scheme proved successful. Passengers lost to the trams came back, traffic doubling in the first year, more than doubling again the next. The LBSCR abandoned plans for the Brighton line, concentrating on suburban services, which by 1912 extended as far as Crystal Palace, Norwood Junction and Selhurst. The First World War cut off supplies of German equipment, so the system was not completed until 1925, by which year the new Southern Railway was standardising on a different system.

The London and North Western Railway (LNWR) also used continental equipment, but of conventional low-voltage technology of German (Siemens) and later Swiss (Oerlikon) make on its suburban lines in north London, which were electrified as part of a wider rebuilding of the main and suburban lines into Euston station. The LNWR electric trains were renowned for comfort and enjoyed by travellers to Watford until replaced in the late 1950s.

13

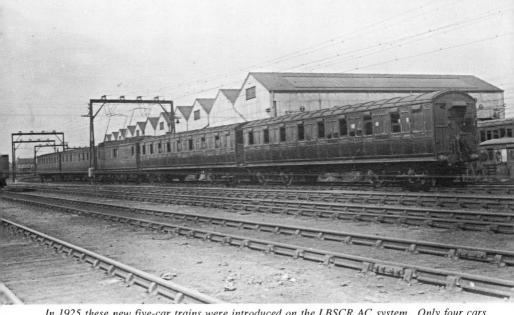

In 1925 these new five-car trains were introduced on the LBSCR AC system. Only four cars carried passengers, the central motor van being a 1000 horsepower locomotive operated by remote control from the outer driving cabs. When the AC scheme was scrapped, these locomotives were rebuilt as heavy brake vans, weighing 27 tons.

The LNWR North London trains were built between 1914 and 1923 by the railway at Wolverton Works and by the Metropolitan Carriage Wagon and Finance Company of Wednesbury, with electrical equipment from Siemens and from Oerlikon of Switzerland. An Oerlikon stock train is seen here on the Harrow service in BR days. The LMS had them in maroon, white and black livery, as on motor coach 28249 in the National Railway Museum.

A Central London Railway 'camelback' locomotive. After replacement by electric cars, most were scrapped but some were sold to industry or, like Underground number 12 shown here, used as shunters. Originally they had a crimson lake livery.

UNITED STATES TECHNOLOGY

In the late 1890s the United States market for electric trains had become overcrowded, and so the price of electric motors fell rapidly. Every major city had its own elevated or underground railway, whilst in the middle of the country a vast network of light 'inter-urban' electric railways connected almost every town and city between Buffalo and Milwaukee in the north, and St Louis and Cincinnati further south. This superb transport network lasted until superseded by roads, most inter-urbans closing in the 1930s.

The electric trains made the suburbs viable. They could make a similar transport revolution abroad. Therefore the American electrical giants, the General Electric Company (GE) and the Westinghouse Company, went abroad. Europe was dominated by German firms, but Britain was an open field for electric railways. So American capital, equipment and men came to Britain.

In particular, they came to London, where the success of the CSLR had inspired many similar ideas, but all had failed for one reason or another. The Americans bought out these unsuccessful schemes and made them work. Between 1895 and 1905 most of central London's present Underground system was built or electrified with American money and equipment.

The first scheme to benefit was the Central London Railway (CLR), a 5.8 mile (9.3 km) underground line from Bank to Shepherd's Bush. Construction began in 1896, the line opening for business in 1900. Like the CSLR, it planned to use locomotives, ordered from GE in America. They were the first electric locomotives exported from the United States. The first passenger paid the fixed fare of 2d on 30th July 1900, and within a few years the 'Tuppenny Tube' was carrying 45 million passengers annually.

However, the company had problems. The tunnel had a peculiar smell, eradicated with new ventilation equipment some years later. Passengers complained that the trains rattled and were cramped. But the greatest

Central London railcar number 212 and trailer, part of the original 68 cars supplied in 1903. They worked until the 1930s, 36 being converted into eighteen electric sleet locomotives in 1939, to clear lines of leaves, snow et cetera. One ESL survived until 1985.

The Metropolitan and District joint experimental electric car, at Earls Court on trials in 1900. It ran between there and Kensington High Street.

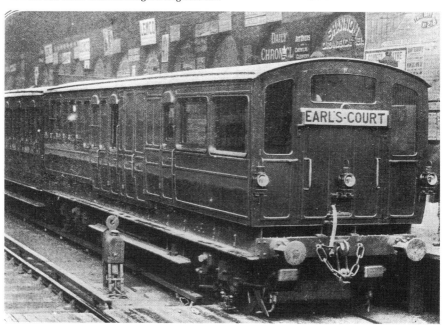

16

problem was the locomotives. They shook the track so severely as to rattle, not only the trains, but all the buildings above the tunnel. Property owners complained, and Board of Trade investigators found in their favour. The locomotives were altered to reduce vibrations, but tests showed that powered carriages, electric multiple units (EMUs), produced only a fraction of the vibrations made by locomotives. They could also carry more passengers. The locomotives were doomed. All thirty were sold. Locomotive-hauled trains have never since been used to carry passengers on the Tube lines. The Tube refers to the deep small tunnels these railways run in.

The new Tubes provided fierce competition for the existing Metropolitan and Metropolitan District Railways. They had opened in the 1860s to work full-size steam trains into central London through shallow tunnels and deep cuttings. Despite the use of 'condensing' engines that consumed

their own steam and smoke, conditions were atrocious. One chemist even sold a 'Metropolitan Mix' to soothe the throats of regular travellers. In the 1860s the Metropolitan had experimented with an electric locomotive, which got stuck in the tunnel, and another one had been tried in the 1880s. Both were battery-powered.

Both 'sub-surface' railways experimented with electric trains in 1900, when about a mile (1.6 km) of track was electrified, but they did not proceed because of a dispute over what system to adopt. As both companies ran trains on each other's track, agreement was vital.

The dispute was settled by C. T. Yerkes, an American financier, who bought the Metropolitan District (District Line) in 1900 and commenced battle with the Metropolitan. The latter preferred a Hungarian-invented AC system; Yerkes wanted an American-style DC system. After extensive pleading with the Board of Trade, his

An 'A' stock train of the South Harrow branch of the District Railway. Note the folding 'Sprague door'. From 1905 420 cars of a similar 'B' stock, but with a central driver's door and two front windows, were used in London.

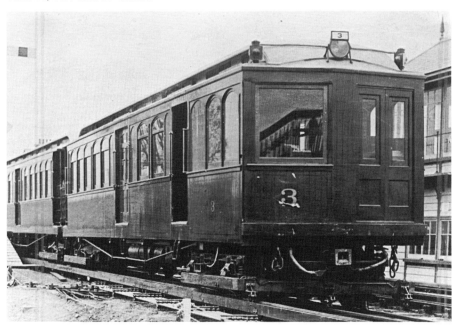

The Tube trains were very similar in design, whether on the Piccadilly, Bakerloo or Hampstead (now Northern) Line. The example shown here is a Hungarian-built car of the Piccadilly Line, in service from 1906. The gate mechanism from one car has been preserved at the London Transport Museum.

Two District Line locomotives leaving Ealing Broadway with a through train to Southend. The electric locomotives were taken off at Barking. The through service ended in 1939.

The Metropolitan Railway later developed a more English style of coachwork, as seen on driving motor car 418, shown here on display.

system was licensed. The 'Battle of the Systems' having been decided, experimental cars were tried on the South Harrow branch, and a standard design was settled upon. This was an American one, though soon both railways adopted distinctive styles, the Metropolitan having a characteristic English look whilst the District always remained rather American. Both companies were used by the main-line railways as routes into and through central London, and to pull such trains locomotives were used, the District having ten ugly little ones, whilst the Metropolitan had two sets of ten, bought before 1914, and replaced after the First World War by twenty new locomotives. Two of these later machines have been preserved.

Having electrified, in every sense of the word, the sub-surface system, Yerkes went on to develop the Tube lines. He completed the projects begun by the Baker Street and Waterloo Railway (Bakerloo), the Hampstead (Northern) and Piccadilly Lines, all opened in 1906-7. Having one owner, and all working in the same conditions, all the lines used similar cars, built in France and Hungary as well as Britain. Usually they had motors built by British Thomson Houston, the British subsidiary of the American General Electric. They, and the later 1923 'standard stock' that replaced them, all had the electrical equipment stored in compartments just behind the driver's cab, and above the axles, so as to provide more weight on the wheels for adhesion. Some of these early Tube trains are preserved at the London Transport Museum, whilst a few of the 1923 stock were put to work in the Isle of Wight until 1989.

British Thomson Houston (BTH) was also responsible for supplying electric trains and equipment to other electric railways, especially the Newcastle suburban lines of the North Eastern Railway (NER). This company was suffering from tramway competition and decided to fight back with new electric trains. Also, one of the biggest power stations in Europe was under construction in Newcastle, and the electricity company was eager to win bulk orders. Railway and power companies came to an

A locomotive of the Metropolitan's original 1904 stock of ten, ordered in 1904, delivered and working from 1906. Note the giant destination blind on its front. Another ten locomotives of a different design were delivered later.

agreement, and work started on electrification in 1902. The new services were introduced in 1904 and proved popular. The hundred original cars were supplemented by another 22 in the First World War, to carry the shipyard workers to their jobs. Though well fireproofed, 34 of the 122 cars were destroyed in a fire at the Walker Gate depot in 1918. They were replaced by 34 new vehicles, also wooden-bodied and of similar design, but with different-shaped roofs.

The NER was unusual in investing in electric locomotives, all designed to use direct current. Two small ones of a standard GE design were used to take freight trains from Newcastle Docks to the main line. They worked from 1904 to 1964, and one is preserved at the National Railway Museum, York.

One of the replacement sets introduced after the Walker Gate depot fire. Wooden-bodied, they had distinctive elliptical roofs.

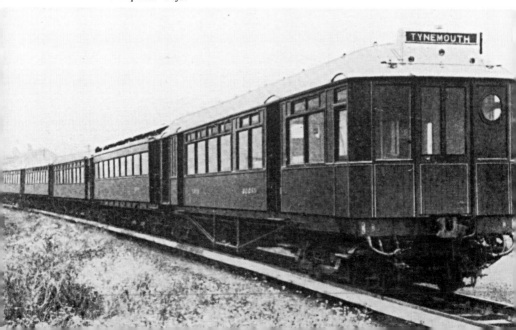

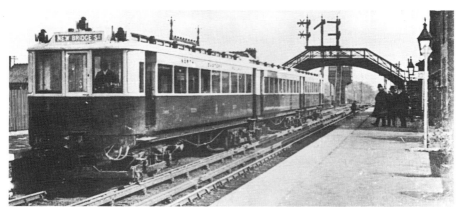

An original North Eastern Railway three-car electric set at Benton station soon after the opening of the service. They had red and cream livery.

Another ten very powerful electric locomotives were bought in 1916, to work on heavy coal trains. Part of the way was over the route of the original Stockton and Darlington Railway. After about twenty years, the line faced heavy bills for renewal of the electric supply equipment. As the coal trade was in recession the then owners, the London and North Eastern Railway (LNER), transferred the line back to steam working. The ten locomotives were stored, but two were reprieved in 1949 to work as shunters in east London, on the newly electrified Shenfield line. They were withdrawn in 1964, and both scrapped.

The NER built two unlucky locomotives, both numbered 13. The first was an experimental engine, a test bed for the proposed third-rail electrification of the Newcastle-York main line. It and the third-rail pro-

The destination blinds were soon taken off the Metropolitan locomotives, as can be seen in this close-up of number 4.

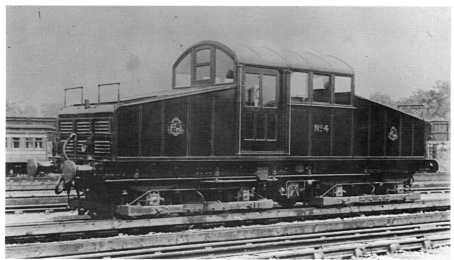

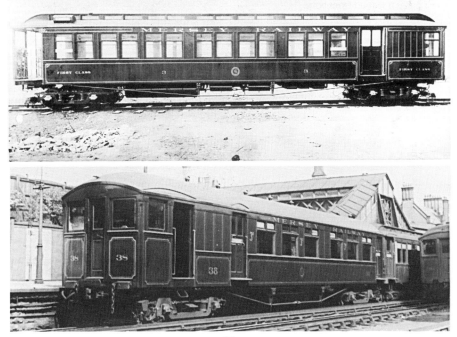

22

posal were scrapped. The NER decided to use overhead wires on the line, and so the second number 13 was built as an express passenger machine taking 1500 volts direct current from overhead wires to be erected on the East Coast main line. She was beautiful and efficient, but financial problems prevented the scheme from being carried out.

GE's great rival, the Westinghouse company, also came to Britain. George Westinghouse, inventor of the air brake and founder of the many Westinghouse companies, built a large factory at Trafford Park, Manchester. British Westinghouse became Metropolitan Vickers in the 1920s, and the Manchester factory is now the home of GEC-Alsthom, one of the largest European makers of electric trains and locomotives. To advertise his railway equipment, Westinghouse electrified the Mersey Railway Company, which ran steam trains through a tunnel under the river Mersey. It did not have the money to electrify, so Westinghouse took payment in shares. When it reopened in 1903, it was the first railway in Britain to have been converted from steam to electric traction. The electric cars used were the first to run as a fleet and were famed for speed. They were assembled at the Westinghouse works in Manchester, from parts made in Shrewsbury to designs supplied by Baldwins of the USA. Until covered over later, the clerestory roofs gave them a distinct 'Wild West' look. Other cars came in the 1920s and 1930s. Some of the original cars ran for fifty years until 1956/7, when they were replaced by British Railways Class 502s. One set was earmarked for preservation and taken into store at Derby, where it was accidentally destroyed by fire.

Facing page, top: *One of the ten Shildon line locomotives in store at South Gosforth shed c.1949, bearing a crudely painted BR number. Most were scrapped in 1950 but one, NER number 11, BR 26510, was used as a shunter at Ilford until 1964.*

Facing page, second from top: *LNER number 13, also in South Gosforth shed, wearing its BR number. It spent most of its life in store, before scrapping in 1950.*

Facing page, second from bottom: *An original Mersey Railway car of 1903, built in Britain using American designs and equipment. Note the distinctive doors and clerestory roof, which give it a definite 'Wild West' look.*

Facing page, bottom: *Mersey Railway motor driving car of post-First World War stock, built by Cravens of Gloucester. An original American-style trailer is attached.*

Below: *NER electric locomotive number 1, the only survivor, shown here outside the National Railway Museum, York, in NER livery.*

23

A train made of 3SUB cars. These three-car suburban sets were old passenger carriages fitted with electric motors. Introduced in 1925, the last one worked in 1949. This photograph shows a train to East Croydon at Tadworth.

INTER-WAR DEVELOPMENTS 1920-31

The great event of the period between the world wars was the development of the south London commuter system, which grew with the suburbs and extended until it reached Brighton and Portsmouth, bringing them within commuting time of London. This system, now operated by British Rail's Network South East, was the world's most heavily used commuter transport system. Major developments also took place on the Underground system, whilst electric services in north London, Merseyside, Glasgow, Manchester and Newcastle were modernised in the same two decades.

The south London system of today has its origins in the London and South Western Railway (LSWR). Like other railways, the company was forced into electrification by competition from tramways, and in this case by potential Underground and rival railway schemes. Herbert (later Sir Herbert) Walker, the most dynamic railwayman of his generation, was appointed General Manager of the LSWR in 1912. After

looking at American railways, the LSWR authorised electrification in 1913.

The first electrified line opened in 1915. It ran from Waterloo to Wimbledon. The 83 three-coach trains were the old steam-pulled carriages of 1904, fitted with electric motors. The driver's cab had a distinctive V-shaped nose and the trains were soon nicknamed 'Torpedoes'. Herbert Walker introduced strict fixed-interval times on this and later services: trains to station X left at 10 past every hour, to station Y at 15 minutes past, and so on. This boosted custom. In 1923 the LSWR, the LBSCR and the South Eastern and Chatham Railway (SECR) amalgamated to form the Southern Railway (SR) under the control of Herbert Walker. The SR possessed two electric systems, the LSWR's 600 volt third-rail DC, and the 6600 volts overhead wire AC of the LBSCR. In 1921 the SECR planned a 1500 volts DC overhead scheme. A decision had to be made to standardise on one system. Whilst the discussions took place the LBSCR scheme was completed, but as the LSWR third-rail system was cheaper to install that was chosen as the standard in 1925.

The overhead system was converted to third rail between 1926 and 1929, and the rolling stock was either adapted to use third rail or scrapped. The AC locomotives had their motors removed and were turned into heavy brake vans for goods trains. By 1930 most suburban lines in south London were electrified on LSWR principles, using third-rail supplied DC current to work trains made up of converted steam-train carriages which left their stations at fixed-interval timings. In the late 1930s the suburban system was extended eastwards into Kent.

In London the Metropolitan, District and London Electric Railway underground systems were modernised and extended in all directions. In 1923 and 1938 new standard designs of Tube vehicles were introduced. The 1923 series had clerestory roofs and looked similar to earlier designs. The London bus and railway companies were amalgamated into the nationalised London Passenger Transport Board in 1933. The new company set to work producing new standard designs. The 1938 Tube trains had underfloor motors for the first time, and many of the comforts of full-size trains. New standard designs were also adopted for the Metropolitan and District systems.

An original 1915 'Torpedo' stock set, the Southern Railway number 1232. Route O was a circular service, Waterloo-Hounslow-Waterloo.

In north London, the London, Midland and Scottish Railway, formed in 1923 by the amalgamation of the LNWR, the LYR, the Midland and some Scottish companies, modernised the rolling stock on its lines. The new EMUs were flat-fronted, rather ugly-looking cars. EMUs of the same type

Electrification made the suburbs, and the suburbs celebrated when the first electric services started. This scene shows the first electric train to arrive at Addiscombe, 28th February 1926. This had been served by the former South Eastern and Chatham Railway. The train set, 3SUB number 1417, was made from old SECR carriages.

Above: *Ex-LBSCR coaches were transformed into two-car 2WIM (for Wimbledon services) and 2SL (Southern Line) sets from 1929, like number 1804, shown here at East Brixton sometime after 1934, before which the 2SL sets were numbered in the series 1901-8. They worked from Victoria on south London routes until withdrawn in the mid 1950s.*

Above: *A 2NOL set number 1840, one of many ordered in 1934, in use by 1936, for local services along the south coast from Brighton and between Waterloo, Windsor and Weybridge. This train service, number 28, was between Reading and Waterloo.*

Below: *A District Railway 'F' stock train of 1920/1. These vehicles were known as 'ovals' or 'salmon tins' from the shape of their front windows. They were amongst the first London trains to have their motors and electrical equipment stored away under the body, instead of in a separate compartment behind the driver, and were the first all-metal trains on the Underground system.*

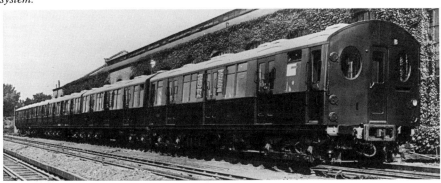

A train of then new 1923 standard Tube stock at Hendon Central station.

were also used in Liverpool, on the LYR system there, until in the 1930s two new types came from the Derby works of the LMSR. The Classes 502 and 503 were very advanced vehicles for their day. The Class 502 worked on the LYR lines to Southport, whilst the Class 503 worked through the Mersey tunnel, sharing duties with the earlier-built Mersey cars, to operate on the newly electrified suburban services in Wirral.

In Newcastle the old (1904) system north of the Tyne was modernised in 1937. The 34 replacement EMUs of 1920 were repainted and put to work on a new line south of the Tyne opened in 1938. The original 1904 cars were scrapped. The heavily used services north of the river were taken over by all-metal cars of a new design. These were unusual for Britain in being articu-lated, that is two cars were permanently joined together, being hinged on a central bogie. The two outer bogies were powered. These double cars ran singly (as two-car sets) but could be coupled in four-car or six-car sets for busy workings. During rush hours they worked as eight-car sets.

The odd design provoked some initial comment from passengers, but the trains soon became popular amongst staff and passengers for comfort and reliability. New trains of Southern Region design came in 1955. From 1963 the Tyneside system was de-electrified, the entire line being dieselised by 1967, though most of the route is now used for the electrified Tyne and Wear Metro. Unfortunately no NER or LNER cars survive, but two NER parcels cars are preserved at York, though one is being moved back to Tyneside for display.

The CLR expanded into the suburbs after 1920 when the Ealing Broadway line was electrified. One of the 1903 trains is seen here on this route in the 1920s. Note the central conductor rail, replaced by the LT standard four-rail system in 1940, and the almost rural scenery.

Experimental streamlined cars were introduced on the Tube in 1935. The streamlining was found to be unnecessary, but it was discovered that the motors could be put away under the body, so releasing space for more passengers. This arrangement was used on the later 1938 standard stock.

New standard Tube stock was introduced in 1938, mainly for use on the Bakerloo and Northern Lines. A four-car train of the Bakerloo Line is shown here. Some of these trains are still in use on the BR system in the Isle of Wight.

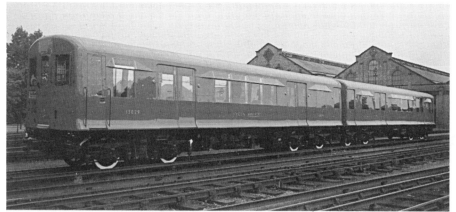

The standard Metropolitan and District trains from 1937 were the 'O', 'P' and 'R' series, all similar in design to this two-car 'O' stock set seen at Ealing Common depot when new in 1937.

In Manchester the LMS and LNER co-operated in electrifying the Manchester, South Junction and Altrincham line. The cars looked ugly. They had the largest motors ever fitted to a British electric train. In Scotland no main lines were electrified in this period, but the formerly cable-worked Glasgow Underground was modernised in 1934, with new electric motors being fitted to the old cars.

There were many plans for main-line electrification, but only the Southern was able to carry them through. The Brighton to London Victoria line was electrified in 1931. A

new luxury express was put on the route, the famous 'Brighton Belle'. From 1937 the electric trains ran to Portsmouth. Britain's first main-line electric locomotive was put into service by the SR in 1940. On the LNER by 1939 work was underway on electrifying the Manchester to Sheffield main line and the suburban line from London to Essex. However, the war stopped all these projects in 1940. They were both completed later after nationalisation in 1948. The new British Railways (BR) decided upon main-line electrification in the 1956 Modernisation Plan. By then a new system had been

A six-car train of standard District design, c.1931. These and similar cars built from 1925 to 1935 were later classified as 'Q' stock.

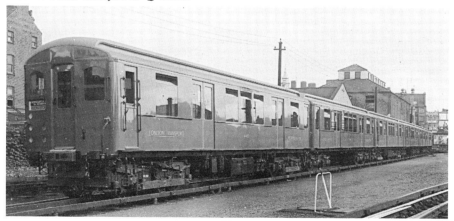

Above: *A 6PAN set, introduced in 1932, with toilets, pantry car and buffet for long-distance passengers on the services from London Victoria to Brighton and Worthing. They were renumbered in 1937, in the series 3021-37. This is number 3025 on the Victoria to Littlehampton route.*

Below: *The three first class only 6-CITY units at London Bridge station c.1937. They ran the top business express services from London to the coast, the evening return departing London at 5.00 for Brighton (service 3), at 5.06 for Worthing (service 17), and at 5.03 for Eastbourne (service 65). The cars were scrapped in the 1960s.*

Below: *The original Brighton to Victoria Pullman service had been steam-hauled and called the 'Southern Belle'. The world's first and only electric all-Pullman train took over after electrification and for a while it too was called the 'Southern Belle', the name carried here by 5BEL unit 2051, c.1932.*

The Southern Railway introduced three large electric locomotives just after 1940, the first, CC1, in 1941, followed by CC2 in 1943. CC3 arrived just after nationalisation in 1948. They had many unique features. CC2 is seen here with a goods train. The class worked mostly on freight duties but also hauled the royal train and boat trains. They were scrapped in 1969.

developed which used high-voltage alternating current (AC). So Britain's main lines use this system. The last important line on the old DC system was the Sheffield to Manchester via Woodhead line, which closed in 1981. However, many suburban lines and the London Underground, as well as the new light railways, such as that in the London Docklands, use the old DC system.

Though only the Southern Railway electrified any long-distance main lines between 1931 and 1940, by 1940 Britain's railways carried more passengers by electric train than any other in the world, owing to the massive traffic carried by the London railways. The electric train was thus partly responsible for developing the suburbs and new towns in the twentieth century.

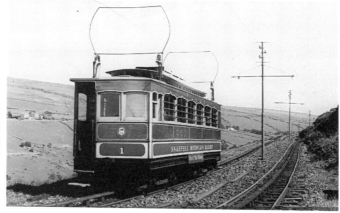

Snaefell Mountain Railway number 1, built in 1895 and still working, though fitted with modern brakes and motors. The Isle of Man is a living museum of steam and electric traction.

31

FURTHER READING

Cooper, B. K. *Electric Trains in Britain.* Ian Allan, 1979.

Gilham, G. C. *The Age of the Electric Train.* Ian Allan, 1988.

Haut, F. J. G. *History of the Electric Locomotive.* Volume I, George Unwin, 1969. Volume II, 'Railcars and the Industrial Locomotive', Tantivy Press, London, 1981.

Marsden, Colin J. *100 Years of Electric Traction.* Oxford Publishing Company, 1985. Profusely illustrated and accurate.

Tassin, Y. Machefert; Nouvion, F.; and Woimant, J. *Histoire de la Traction Electrique*, tome I, 'Dès Origines à 1940'. La Vie du Rail, Paris, 1980. The standard work on early electric trains throughout the world; in French and very expensive but worth ordering from a library because of its many excellent and rare prints and maps.

Vickers, R. L. *DC Electric Trains and Locomotives in Britain.* David and Charles, 1986.

PLACES TO VISIT

There are displays of electric locomotives and railcars at the following museums. Intending visitors are advised to find out the opening times before making a special journey. In addition, London Underground 1938 stock cars now work on British Rail's Isle of Wight line (Ryde to Shanklin).

Glasgow Museum of Transport, Kelvin Hall, 1 Bunhouse Road, Glasgow G8 8PZ. Telephone: 041-357 3929. Glasgow subway stock.

Liverpool Museum, William Brown Street, Liverpool, Merseyside L3 8EN. Telephone: 051-207 0001. Liverpool Overhead Railway car and memorabilia.

London Transport Museum, 39 Wellington Street, Covent Garden, London WC2E 7BB. Telephone: 071-379 6344.

Museum of Science and Industry, Liverpool Road Station, Liverpool Road, Castlefield, Manchester M3 4JP. Telephone: 061-832 2244.

National Railway Museum, Leeman Road, York, North Yorkshire YO2 4XJ. Telephone: 0904 62161.

Ramsey Electric Railway Museum, Manx Electric Railway Station, Ramsey, Isle of Man. The electric system on the island uses original 1890s cars (with new motors and brakes).

Ulster Folk and Transport Museum, Cultra Manor, Holywood, County Down, Northern Ireland BT18 0EU. Telephone: 0232 428428.

SOCIETY

Electric Railway Society: Honorary Secretary, Dr I. D. O. Frew, 17 Catherine Drive, Sutton Coldfield, West Midlands B73 6AX.

The all-Pullman express was renamed the 'Brighton Belle' in 1934, and the three sets were renumbered 3051-3 in 1937. They worked until 30th April 1972. Car 3051, formerly 2051, is seen here as the 'Brighton Belle'.